The World is Ending and Maybe That's Kinda Hot

A drunk adaptation of "The Decameron" by Boccaccio

By Catherine Weingarten

Uproar Theatrics

LICENSING & PRODUCTION INQUIRIES
Uproar Theatrics, LLC.
hello@uproartheatrics.com | www.UproarTheatrics.com

CHARACTERS (5W, 3M)

The Ladies (4W)
Filomena
headstrong, dating Panfilo, you wanna be her.
Emilia
super sexy, really spacey, is so intriguing you can't stop thinkin about it.
Lauretta
really bad at writing songs, kinda a mopey chick, obsessed with Filostrato.
Pampinea
super wide-eyed, little bit dumb, really into Dioneo which means she has bad taste in men.

The Gents (3M)
Panfilo
super sweet, can be a doormat, is too nice to be on Tinder.
Filostrato
Kinda an intense dude, perpetually bitter about his exes, has separation anxiety from his dog.
Dioneo
Supa lusty, likes bird watching, doesn't give an F.

The Patron Saints (1W)
Clarita*
Patron saint who kinda sucks at it.

*Note-all these characters are between the ages of late teen-late 20s and can be played of actors of any race.

*Note: Clarita can be played by a puppet or some other theatrical trick.

-
-

SETTING

A super good looking field where everything is green and fricking calming.

TIME

14th Century Italy…for real

Note on set-

The play takes place in an idyllic pasture. But this world is a little weirder and more theatrical, so feel free to play with more contemporary and odder touches like for example one tree is made with pink glitter leaves. Also note when the stories are told there does not need to be an elaborate set change, they can just be told in a simple barebones way.

Note on Scene Titles-

The scene titles should be projected or incorporated in some cool way so the audience can tell what day it is and also they help add some flavor!

A Note on Format and Language

The reader will instantly notice the unique format of the script. The language eschews standard spelling, grammar, and line breaks, and all are deliberate personal choices and are done to emphasize character and emotional truth. I am influenced by e.e cummings and his unconventional spelling and punctuation, as well as how millennials use language and textspeak.

Notes for Actors

General Note-

The characters in my plays will do anything to achieve what they want. Even though it's a comedy, really connect to something truthful without commenting or getting too sitcomy.

Language Index

Line breaks- Think of this like Shakespearean verse, it is
done to help show the rhythm of the way I see the line. Let it
guide you but do not let it overpower or become too obvious.
(Parentheses) = it means it's a more internal line and more
hushed.
Words abbreviated = do not unabbreviated, like if the script
says "wtf" just say those three letters
Misspellings= honor the word as written, there's some
language play going on so just embrace it
Emoticons= don't speak them, they are used as a nonverbal
emotional heightened moment of feeling, play around!

Out of fear and shame, women keep the flames of love
hidden within their delicate breasts, and as everyone knows
who has had this experience, such fires have much greater
force than do those that burn out in in the open… And, if
because of these thoughts, a fit of melancholy brought on by
their burning desire should take possession of their minds, it
will inevitably remain there, causing them great pain, unless
it is removed by new interests. Finally, women's power of
endurance are simply less than those of men.

-Introduction of "The Decameron," Boccaccio (trans. Wayne
Rebhorn)

Prologue: Tell me a Hot story

PAMPINEA

It's so hard, like um so hard and stuff, like all
Day I just sit in my barn and milk cows
Who look depressed and I stare out a small window
And I see the world and it's glittering
And yet I'm just stuck.
And all I can think about is;
Like I just want a hot story,
I want someone to tell me a story that makes me
Pass out,
That makes my face look like an organic tomato;
And I know girls are supposed to just experience life like
A piece of hot cardboard, but maybe I'm different ok??
And it's like
It's like, stories,in general,
Are so hot? But then..when they're supposed to be hot!?
(OMG)
It's like the story starts so innocently
Like so slowly
Like creeping up on you, telling you
Who's who, who has the goal,
And then it like Rampss UP-and starts moving faster
And then the protagonist like fucking does something
And it's so hot! Like human achievement..mmm
And then it all gets wrapped up
And it's a happily ever after but hotter
And I cool down.
And I think back on that,
I just feel like a good story can like
Make you immortal and stuff like,
Like everyone's dying right now
But like if you tell stories you can't,
And your stories can't.
Like when I hear a good story ma bod

PAMPINEA (cont)
Lights up like a Ms.Pacman machineee
The only kind of stories my mom tells me
Are about runaway ducks…and lost ducks…
There's nothing hot about being a lost duck….

Day 1-That plague was lame

> *(A group of girls and guys sit on a field. They*
> *look super prim and fancy, like someone your*
> *mom would try to set you up with.)*

FILOMENA

Wow, that plague was so lame, like ew.
Likee
So glad we ran away,
Like so many randos kept dying.

PAMPINEA

You're so obserrrvant, Filomena.
Like great observation.
Ya, it was like really hard like
My seven siblings died..and ma mom.
Oh well.
Like I'm fine and shittt… :/
It's so nice to be here with you guys.
Like we neva get together enough.

PANFILO

We really don't, Pampinea.
Ya,I'm glad the Black Death can bring us all together,
Even if it brings some further apart.

EMILIA

So deep yaaa

FILOMENA

You're so deep.
Like that's rare to find in a dude.

*(PANFILO and FILOMENA makeout as
PAMPINEA kinda cries and others look.)*

FILOSTRATO

I think my guinea pig Pompeii may have died…
I know noblemen shouldn't care about that kinda shit…
But I do?????
(Is something wrong with meeeeee?)

FILOMENA

Nothing's wrong with you Filostrato, you're just more
Sensitive
Than most, which is kinda weird but also ok.

FILOSTRATO

Thank you kind ladyyy.

LAURETTA

I think um my guinea might have died too..
So-that's-cool(something in common? For us?)
Maybe they're hanging in guinea heaven?
Like knocking em back? Knocking back the guinea
whiskey?
Telling stories about us?

FILOSTRATO

Guinea pigs don't drink alcohol…
At least mine didn't. Don't know what you fed yours…

LAURETTA

It was um
Rhetorical?
He was lucky to have you as a pet owner though…

FILOSTRATO

Um thanks.

EMILIA

You were kinda like a bad pet owner Lauretta,
Like who feeds guineas Frosted Flakesss?
Like just cause you like them doesn't mean they're-like
Suitableee for animal consumption.

LAURETTA

But they're more than good, they're GREAT!

*(Everyone seems upset by the thought of
LAURETTA owning a pet. Weird moment.)*

EMILIA

Like how long we gunna stay here though??
Cause I left all my good jewels at home,
And I have like
Separation anxiety from them.
I have a pair of pink jewels
And sometimes I like stare at myself wearing them
In the mirror for like
Hours.
It's like fascinating.

DIONEO

Could I watch sometime?

EMILIA

Like they look relly good on me
Ughhhsss
Sometimes beauty is but a blessing
And sometimes it is but a curse.

PAMPINEA

I promised I'd give my guinea pig a proper guinea funeral
Sooo....................

FILOSTRATO

We'll stay here as long
As the plague rage-eth on.
That's the only way to guarantee our safety.
Is everyone ok with that?

EVERYONE (at differing times)

Kk kewl
Ugh fuck
This field is cool
You suck
Your girlfriend's too hot for you

FILOMENA

That's really smart Filostrato,
Like you're so smart sometimes I can't even tell if you're
Like a real person.

DIONEO

This vague looking pastoral field is so pretty
Ya know?
Like something so soothing about it like
Makes me forget everything that ever came before it
And our city is just like crawling with rabid guinea pigs and
Rats and dying ugly people and like uckkkk
Like it's a lot!
And like we have money and stuff, like doesn't that mean
We deserve betttter?
Like like a new life,

FILOMENA

That's really deep Dioneo, yaaasss
Like we rellly
Shouldn't have to deal wit this shit…
Like we each so rich!

PANFILO

Good point honey face…
I do possess riches
But my greatest riches in life
Are yo face.
Your hair is so lush and full
A man and his whole family could
Drown a horrible death in it…in a hot way.

FILOMENA

I think I'm crying…
No I'm ok.

PAMPINEA

Wow, it is so beautiful here,
Look at all the pretty olive trees
And the sun looks like an old friend
You want to sit underneath with a potential lover
Sit under some lush ferns and talk of one's dreams
And wishes,
Doesn't that sounds nice, Dioneo?

DIONEO

I guess...

PAMPINEA

What do you dream of in the even Dioneo?

DIONEO

Umm...well made bread?
Not burnt in the slightest.

PAMPINEA

I love that...

DIONEO

Thanks....
So ummm...what should we do now...
To pass the time?
Naked poker? Naked four square? Naked hot dog eating contest?

LADIES (each one says a different response)

Ewwwww!
That's offensive to me!
Calm it down!
Ma hamster just died and I'm in a vulnerable place

FILOMENA

I'd prefer to have my clothing on...

LADIES

Yaaaaaaa

DIONEO

Why don't we tell stories or something?
To pass the time?
And we can enlist eachother to help tell the tales?

PAMPINEA

I once played a tree in a school pageant
And it was such fun!

EMILIA

I can see you possesing the magnetism
To embody a tree!

FILOMENA

I think that sounds like a splendid way
To pass the time!
Panfilo and I love to attend the theater
And throw stones when it does not pleaseth us!

PANFILO

Yaaaa

FILOSTRATO

You really shouldn't throw stones
At actors.
They are already harlots and the scum of society,
Would be kinder to support their sad playacting
And speak badly of them
In the comfort of your own mansion.

FILOMENA

Well maybe I disagreeth.

FILOSTRATO

(well maybe you're hot!)

FILOMENA

Did you say something?

PANFILO

I love the theater!
Especially when they have live lions
On the stage and they eat the worst actors!
What fun!

LAURETTA

Oooo
And when we tell stories,
I can even add in some live music!!

DIONEO

So we're all in agreement then??

ALL

Sooo into it

PAMPINEA

I told my guineas stories all the time
And they always looked quite pleased.
Ok, gather round now everyone.

EMILIA

Oh, I'll go!
I have a really good one...
I shall play Feather
And Pampinea will you play Giusepetta?
Because like I think it's your "type."

PAMPINEA

Sure!

(EMILIA gives PAMPINEA her script.)

EMILIA

So once upon a time there lived
A young beautiful girl named Giusepetta
And her maid, Feather.

PAMPINEA (as GIUSEPETTA)

And Feather and I were super tight like
wherever I would go,
she would go with me!
She was so whipped!
Like suriously I would go to the bathroom
And she would ask to come along,

PAMPINEA (as GIUSEPETTA, cont)

That was a little weirder than her usual requests but who
knows…
So one day I come home and I have the most
Excitinggg news to share!
"Listen sweet Feather, so like
I was milking and stuff like normal
Like not even like cute milking,
Like average chick basic bitch milking,
Which like I usually don't do but you're so bad at it,
I just thought it would make your chores
Go faster and stuff
And so this GUY approaches and just says,
Out of nowhere
"wow, your milking skills are above average,
I'm Gipette."
And then we talked for sooo long
And I learned how his mother was so mean growing up
And his baby brother's cuteness is overrated
And then he left but he said he would come back
And see me again and I can'ttttt
Stop thinking about him!
Oh sweet Feather! My dear servant Feather!
How lucky a lady am I???
To meet a fine gentleman at random!

EMILIA (as FEATHER)

Hmmm
He sounds kinda weird tho…

PAMPINEA (as GIUSEPETTA)

Weird! I think not! More like hot as F!
He was so hot he could melt the sun in an instant!
Gurlllll
I think I'm crying, no I'm good

EMILIA (as FEATHER)

Whatever
Men are overrated like as a sex
I think
Like all they do is like kill animals
And like provide us with food everyday
And like build us homes with their bare hands!
Like so lameeeee....over it. Don't need emmm

PAMPINEA (as GIUSEPETTA)

Feather! No! Don't say such
Words as those! If I could
 I would pluck them out of your mouth
And set them to flames!

EMILIA (as FEATHER)

Noo don't set them aflameee
I sorry!

PAMPINEA (as GIUSEPETTA)

He sounds a little yummy right??

EMILIA (as FEATHER)

Sure...
I just don't think you need a man to make you happy,
You are such a resourceful lady
With all the promise in the world
And blush of youth in your cheeks.

PAMPINEA (as GIUSEPETTA)

I hope I see him tomorrow EEEK!
And all day long I would talk about this man
And mentions lots of random
facts about his childhood.
Alas, there was no way for us to contact each other,
Cellphones did not exist then,
They still don't which sucks

PAMPINEA (as GIUSEPETTA, cont)
Cause we could legit be on facebook this whole time
Instead of talking to each other
But I'm getting distracted,
So everyday I sat and waited and smiled
And waited for him.
But little did I know Feather had a big secret
And the waiting
could potentially be fruitless…

EMILIA (as FEATHER)
I don't know if he's gunna come back,
I'm sorry Giusepetta.
You deserve everything you ever wanted,
When you catch a chill, I wish I could become the warmth,
When you are hot, I wish I could be an igloo
For you to rest your weary head instead.
When you are sad, I wish I could be a chipper Britney Spears concert
To comfort your woes!
Oh Alack Alack Alack!
That one can just be mortal and not be mother nature herself
When needed.

PAMPINEA (as GIUSEPETTA)
Sorry was spacing out-wahhhhhhh!
I miss him sooo!
Hmm your hair looks a little messy today,
And that will reflect badly on me!
I care about ma rep!
Ugh the sun has set, it is time to slumber,
You can go now Feather.
I will wait in solitude.
Oh Feather, wait just a second,
Do you think Gipette will appear tomorrow?

EMILIA (as FEATHER)

Probs not…

PAMPINEA (as GIUSEPETTA)

Why so bleak Feather?
Why would you think such a sad thought?

EMILIA (as FEATHER)

I dunno,
Like it's really no bigs
But I might have pushed him down a mountain
Like when I saw him waiting for you one time?

PAMPINEA (as GIUSEPETTA)

WAAAAAAAAA

EMILIA (as FEATHER)

I just, I, I It was for your own good
Like I had reasons

PAMPINEA (as GIUSEPETTA)

And what reasonsss are those?

EMILIA (as FEATHER)

Well um, ugh I cannot say,
But good ones!

PAMPINEA (as GIUSEPETTA)

Oh Feather you are so foolish! Oh WOAH IS MEEEEE
he was my one true love! And his backstory
Was SO interesting!
You are legit insane!
I thought you were but a humble serving wench,
Not a woman gone mad!
Gurl you u crae!

EMILIA (as FEATHER)

No my lady,
I am not that word "crae",
It's just
You are all I think about:
Serving you, helping you, being with you,
How you make the bed so well
After I make it mediocrely
And those sweet words of torment you fling at me
Become so sexy
From your lips, your perfect red lips.
Oh Giuseptta! Please let me kiss you!

PAMPINEA (as GIUSEPETTA)

But I don't understand…
Men kiss women... that's just how the world spinneth!
That's what my parents told me!
I mean, what are you implying?

EMILIA (as FEATHER)

Just don't overthink it. Gender is but a construct,
Why should we just do what we are supposed to do?
I find that boring.

PAMPINEA (as GIUSEPETTA)

Wow, I never thought about it like that.
Everything is but a construct!
My life is but a construct
Wow, you really care about me

(EMILIA kisses PAMPINEA.)

EMILIA

And Feather and Giusepetta began a secret love affair
that was super-hot
But they never told anyone about it
Cause it was illegal. The end!

PANFILO

Wowwww…..that ending.

DIONEO

I think that was uhhh
I think that was the best story
I've ever heard in my whole life

FILOSTRATO

Ya like um you deserve a medal or something,
Like ENCORE.

EMILIA

Aw thanks guys! You're so supportive!

PAMPINEA

I found the ending a bit abrupt.
Also did you use your tongue?

EMILIA

That's like how stage kisses work…

PAMPINEA

oh

FILOMENA

Did she really kill him though? Like he
Sounded pretty interesting.
What an interesting backstory.

PAMPINEA

Dioneo, would you like to go on a nightly stroll with me,
Tell me more of your thoughts??? :)

DIONEO

No.

(Shift: Fantasy Sequence with PAMPINEA and FANTASY DIONEO)

PAMPINEA

If it was just him and me,
This is what he'd say:

DIONEO

I noticed you

PAMPINEA

Yaaa???

DIONEO

No one else knows how to tell her maid how to chop carrots
like you...
Like that tone in your voice..
Like you kinda hate your life...

PAMPINEA

Yaa??

DIONEO

Oh, ya..
The next story I tell, it's gunna be like so inappropriate
Like everyone's faces will look like
Organic beets and I'm gunna be thinking about you
The whole time I tell it....every second...

PAMPINEA

Do you think about me at night? Do you think about me
when it's so dark you can't even feel your toes? How about
when your mom is yelling at you to get your shit together
and that your facial hair sucks?
Do I get into your mind?

DIONEO

Yes, yes and yes.

PAMPINEA

I have a long distance boyfriend in Canada...
does that scare you??

DIONEO

No, it is erotic to me.

PAMPINEA

Oh, cool. Well I'd dump him anyway like if you wanted me to,
like even for a split second
 you considered it.

DIONEO

Ok, good to know.

PAMPINEA

You're good to know. Tell me what would happen
if you could do anything,
where would you kiss me, what would happen?

DIONEO

I'd put my fingers in your hair and it would
Sprout daisies and shit
And with one touch of my hand
Your whole body would feel like a Care bears friendly rainbow
Of joy
And your breath would spin pink and blue cotton candy;
I would not be able to take my hands off of you..

PAMPINEA

Wow, ya, that sounds so cool!
Oh fantasy Dioneo you are so hot and
So much easier to talk to than the real Dioneo.

DIONEO

I try.

PAMPINEA

Tell me what to do so he'll notice me!
Tell me WHAT to do to make things happen!

DIONEO

…
He likes Emilia…

PAMPINEA

Why? Cause she's prettier than me? Cause she's like
Richer than me or always looks so hot
When she spaces out…

DIONEO

Probably all those reasons..but I don't know?

PAMPINEA

Kkkkkkk. Can I make out with you for a while,
while I cry?
Is that weird?

DIONEO

No, that doesn't sound weird at all.

Day 2- Stop annoying me ugh!

FILOMENA

You eva just feel so annoyed like cause your servant is justttt
like
Cleaning your house
But just like soo slowly?
And like it's hard to like
Sew or hang wit your friends
Or anythinggg
Cause she's just there?

EMILIA

Ya, blah
I hate that. My servant Mona,
Sometimes like takes three-hour long smoke breaks
Which is already bad,
And I can see like big puffs
Of pink smoke from the window
And it's like making the air outside ma house
Like slightlyyyy
Less enjoyable??
And nice smelling
For others....

PAMPINEA

My goats like piss me off SO MUCH
Sometimes...
Likeee..my DAD got us the most EXPENSIVE
Expensive ass goats he can find and like they still
Sometimes kick me in the face
While I'm in the bathroom
(Whas up with that?!!!!!?)
(NOT COOL!?!)

FILOMENA

That's a little off topic...but I'm sorry to hear about that

PAMPINEA

I don't think it was...

FILOMENA

It relllly wassss.

PAMPINEA

Your so mean ugggg,
Like stop Cyber Bullying me not on the interwebbbb

EMILIA

It's ok Pampinea,
You be as off topic as you want,
A lady's mind is as wondering as a tumbleweed
Who is but drunk...

LAURETTA

It was kinda off topic though....
But whatevsss
Sometimes my servant like folds
Ma clothes so sloppily and then I just like take a broom
And hit her in the face.
Like so hard
I can feel it...
It's cool cause it's a disciplining action yet ALSOO
Great cardio for the arms!

PAMPINEA

So educational!

EMILIA

Ugh I have the worst muscle tone

PAMPINEA

I can relate to that

EMILIA

Ya reallyzz???
I don't think so…

FILOMENA

Sames..
Oo I actually have the fattest pile of straw behind my house
When we home we could use that as weights???

PAMPINEA

OMG YAY!!!

LAURETTA

Is it bad everyone is dying and we just talking about
Our servant's failure at living?
Like should we be doing somethinggg?
Like signing a change.org petition
Or like donating a sock to charity?

FILOMENA

We young women Lauretta,
We gots to do ussss
Like YOLO
Like we're A-LIVE,
Like we have 2 arms and 2 legs and
We attractive…
It'll all work outtt.

LAURETTA

Ugh I just miss it so bad though,
Like being at home, like being mean to servants.
My core is legit sufferinggg…

FILOMENA

No, we are all fine, calm it down.
Now let's go like tell stories in a hot way
And listen in a hot way
And breathe in a hot way
And make the guys like us more.

OTHER LADIES

Kkkkkk
I'm obsessed with you
Why isn't weight watchers invented yet?
You're so wise
I'm so good at listening

(All men enter and everyone gathers round.)

FILOSTRATO

Oh, it is my turn to tell a story!
Let me!

FILOMENA

Sure, it like doesn't really matter the order or anything.

LAURETTA

Oh I cannot wait for your story Filostrato!
I've been waiting for this day for so long,
I shall take so many mental snapshots during
And describe them after
Since you don't have the immense full body
Pleasure of getting to hear the story
You tell us!

FILOSTRATO

Dearest ladies and gentleman,
Gather round and hear a story
about a love-struck servant so

FILOSTRATO (cont)
Love struck he did something that could have gotten him
killed,
But he was so hot, so whatevers.
I shall play the humble servant,
Filomena will you play the Wife?
Since that part requires a beauteous young lady!

EMILIA
Is that a burn to the rest of us??

FILOSTRATO
Uhhh
No.
And Panfilo, can you take on the small part
Of the husband?

PANFILO
Oh I would love to perform!
No one has asked me yet.

*(FILOSTRATO gives scripts to FILOMENA and
PANFILO and they prepare.)*

FILOSTRATO (as SERVANT)
The king's wife is just so hot,
Like I don't know what to do about it,
Like I've never seen a lady with hair so radiant
And breath that smells like a Victoria Secret's catalogue
And it's like:
She'll-ride a horse and-like
She becomes like like a goddess,
Like she's too good for that horse,
That horse can suck it,
(if only I was that horse),
But alack, her husband is my master!
And he has such a sucky beard, like I'm sorry some men just

FILOSTRATO (as SERVANT, cont)
Should NOT grow beards, ya feel me??
There must be something I can do to win her hand!
Hmm oh I forgot I have no money and therefore no
prospects
So guess I can never win her hand…
That's a downer…
Wait but there's at least something I can do
To be with her!
I will dress as the king and have intercourse with her…
Like a bed trick!
Everyone looks the same in the bedroom, duhhh!
What an amazing idea…. You can really tell I
Went to medieval servant boys entrepreneurial dream big
summer camp!
So I come into her bedroom
And it feels like I've died, like it's so perfect
Like everything has gold and diamonds on it
And there's a big painting of her lacking clothes…
Which I shall not object to
and she's lying in bed and
she's snoring a little and surprisingly
I'm into it!
It's hot!
And the snores get louder and I approach her and
Touch her cheek and her cheek feels like
The Botanical Garden but like on steroids.

FILOMENA (as WIFE)
I'm really into sleeping, like I like at least
12 hours
Cause there's nothing else to do
During the day when you're a queen,
Except like throw cans at servants who sucks or
Pet expensive birds my husband buys for me
And suddenly this man wakes me up,
He is dressed exactly like my husband

24

FILOMENA (as WIFE, cont)
but I know who he is immediately,
He's my hottest servant, like his body is but
A wonderland, but then I remember he is poor
And that
Is offensive to me,
But he also has nice dimples like Hallmark
Movie worthy dimples like start a new life
Worthy dimples,
And I think he thinks I think he's my husband,
Which is dumb AF, like I've been married to the same lame dude
For 10 years so, I know what he looks like,
But I'll just go along with it...

FILOSTRATO (as SERVANT)
And I touch her and our bodies
Communicate like little song birds
Saying hi over different branches
and it's just perfect

FILOMENA (as WIFE)
And in modern times this would be offensive,
In modern times someone would write a feminist tweet about this
That would be retweeted so many timesss,
But it's not modern times, soo...
Also sometimes my husband is so boring I fall asleep at him
Cause he talks about land and land shares
And moats and boring shit like that
And when he kisses me I just feel blank.
And when this servant kisses me (oops don't know his name),
I feel like firecrackers dipped in lemonade and
And expensive chocolates in a tornado
And maybe this is so hot
Or-maybe-this-is-so-offensive and I can't tell

FILOMENA (as WIFE, cont)
And I'll replay it over and over again later
And won't be able to ever know.

FILOSTRATO (as SERVANT)
And after it's done I leave,
But it's so hard cause I have so many questions:
"How did it feel?"
"How Big am I?"
"Will you go on a tantric yoga retreat with mee cause I got a
deal on groupon?"
But I can't ask those questions,
I shouldn't ask those questions
So I just go.
And that's it.

FILOMENA (as WIFE)
And then my husband comes in
And I rely on that hot chicks ancient acting class
I took a few summers ago and dial it UPPPP!
"Why would you come back in so soon after leaving
Dearest, perfectest husband of mine eye??"

PANFILO (as HUSBAND)
And when she says that I know something has happened,
Something so dark even the darkest coffee drinkers
Would spit it out.
And I know someone drank her
like an extra-large bottle of Red Bull
before an all nightery
and I know that she can't tell the difference
because she is a woman aka pretty dumb
and that everyone looks the same in the dark.
So I leave but I'm like SO so pissed
And I go down to the servant's quarters
and I look for the man sleeping with his heart beating
too fast,

PANFILO (as HUSBAND, cont)
and out of all the servants I finally find him
and cut off a bit of his hair
to remember it was him who did that to my fair wife.
I could kill him that even
But I am possessed with a feisty tiredness
And don't want to have bad dreams
Cause I am prone to them,
And will wait till tomorrow.

FILOSTRATO (as SERVANT)
And he cuts off my hair and I know I'm done for,
Like this is it, so I decide to cut off a bit of
Everyone's hair so he can't tell the difference
And it works and
The next day the king can't tell who did it
Since all our hair looks v bad
And like I can't believe it, like I am so fricking smart,
But I guess not smart enough to talk to her again or
Even look at her,
did she know it was me?
I hope she did, but women are dumb so probs not.

FILOMENA (as WIFE)
And it never happens again,
But I still think about him,
What his muscles feel like, the way he tilts his head,
The way he sweeps the floor like he's in a Britney spears
Music video
And every time I get sad,
I get sad for all the lives I never lived, could have lived.

FILOSTRATO (as SERVANT)
And I never talk to the king's wife again,
But in my dreams, we are together,
In my dreams our daughter is gluten free and has
A lisp, a cute one too not the debilitating kinda one

FILOSTRATO (as SERVANT, cont)
And our life together
is perfect and shit, like so perfect

LAURETTA
OMG WHAT A STORY!

(LAURETTA gives FILOSTRATO a standing
ovation.)

PAMPINEA
I found it a bit crude :(

DIONEO
A lady must find everything crude or she is not
Truly a lady.

LADIES
Touche!

(Later that Day. FILOMENA is alone and
FILOSTRATO approaches her.)

FILOSTRATO
Panfilo smiles too much for a dude.
Don't know why you're with him.

FILOMENA
That's sexism…Men can smile as much as they want.

FILOSTRATO
Srryyyy :/

FILOMENA

It's stupid but like,
Some people in ma fam like kept talking about
throwing us a wedding,
like once Panfilo proposes
Like high on a hilltop,
With like lots of goats surrounding us
Like wearing flowers and maybe little bridal
Veils…nothing's cuter than goats in clothing.

FILOSTRATO

Has he proposed or something??

FILOMENA

No…but he will….
He says we're too young…
But like wtf does that mean.
Like the point of life is to get married…
Like why do I have to be 90 to do it?

FILOSTRATO

Youth is but a construct.

FILOMENA

Right??? Yaaaa

FILOSTRATO

Can I tell you a secret?

FILOMENA

Ya,duh.

FILOSTRATO

I wanted to marry my ex, Sarsaparilla, remember her?
Bar maid chick who always looked sad?

FILOMENA

Ooo I think I blocked that out.

FILOSTRATO

She said she would marry me but then she fucking dumped me
for some random rich priest
who hit on her at a bar and took her to Milan
or somewhere dumb like that...

FILOMENA

That's awful! I'm so sorry!

FILOSTRATO

You should be, she was the fucking worst.
I liked her so much even just,
Like thinking about her I want to throw that melon
Over there off the hill...
Is that weird?
Like maybe it'll roll into Milan and hit
her in the face?
That would be nice...

FILOMENA

Oh, please don't Filostrato!
That's a delightful melon tree,
We're actually friends, I named it Melly!

FILOSTRATO

That's not too creative of you.
That name is pretty basic.

FILOMENA

Well women don't go to school in this time period
So sorry for living!

FILOSTRATO

I didn't mean that… I think it's a cute name…
I think everything about you is so special
except your pot smoking bf
whose too happy to be a normal man.

FILOMENA

We shouldn't be having this conversation…

FILOSTRATO

Come onnnn,
We on va-cae!! Story themed vacae!
Do you ever think about…
What do you think would happen
If we
Touched?

FILOMENA

No, course not. Ladies don't think about stuff like that,
We think about friendly looking birds
And um handmaid pies and shit.

FILOSTRATO

I think if I touched you we would both explode,
Like become a million fragments
Like a glitter bath bomb from Lush
In everyone's faces,
Like blinding them forever.
Bsshhh!

FILOMENA

I should go.
We shouldn't talk-again for a while, I don't think.

(Shift-later that day.)

PAMPINEA

I can't wait for you to tell a story,
You're just gunna be so much better than everyone elseee

DIONEO

Thanks man.

PAMPINEA

Like even you just talking,
Like even a small anecdote and tis
Life changing,
You just have such gusto, like so professional-y
Like you could be a professional storyteller
Or something fancy like that.

DIONEO

There are a lot of feral cats near my place and I
Sometimes tell them stories…
So guess I'm well practiced.

PAMPINEA

I wish I was better at telling stories…
Maybe I should stop by your place sometime
And practice with the cats too?

DIONEO

They'd probs bite you though…they only like men…

PAMPINEA

Oh well, well it's ok,
No need to think about your old home,
We are all somewhere new now,
Somewhere with lush trees birthing fruit
And cicadas that hum cutely
And sometimes even hum happy birthday,
When you smile at them widely enough,
Isn't that nice?

DIONEO

....

PAMPINEA

Where do you um get your inspiration?

DIONEO

I'm inspired so easily,
So-really like anything:
A fat cloud, a feral cat gnawing at my ear in the even,
A sexy look from a lady.

PAMPINEA

What um would you define as a sexy look?

DIONEO

Ha how about I show you?
(DIONEO does a sexy look that would ignite a forest fire.
PAMPINEA might have just died…I'm not sure…ugh I hope
she's ok cause I do like that character!)

DIONEO

You wanna try now?

PAMPINEA

Uh sure..ya ok..I'm fine with that…if you are?
But sure.
Don't know if I could live up to that…
But trying is important!

DIONEO

Just squint your eyes together a little,
Now pout your mouth(ya that's good),
Then just look a little angrier,
Perfect!

PAMPINEA

Wow, I feel so physically attractive to the opposite sex.

DIONEO

That's the goal.

PAMPINEA

Oh Dioneo: you're so sassy and it seems like
You don't listen to anybody:
What does that feel like? To be so free?

DIONEO

I don't know-liberating?

PAMPINEA

What do I seem like? Do I seem like that?

DIONEO

You seem like someone that's never been kissed.
You seem like someone who couldn't climb a ladder easily.
You seem like someone who never thinks what kind of milk
is her favorite,
like you kinda like 2% but you so ambivalent?
You seem like someone who looks at the stars so long her
eyes hurt, you seem like someone who is waiting,
you seem like someone who enjoys vegan mac n cheese,
you seem like someone who doesn't know what her body
feels like,
you seem like someone who could fall in love seven times in
an hour, you seem like a seashell,
you seem special
yet like something never meant
to be near
me.

Day 3-Sexual tension is fun in the right context!

PAMPINEA

Do you think it's like bad we're here?
Like are we like selfish or something?
Like my baby-sitter got stolen by a pirate
And a lot of people died of bleeding
And angst and I just watched them,
Cause like I don't have healing experience
Or whatever, but like were we supposed to learn it?
To acquire it?
I just feel like maybe we should have stayed there
And figured it out.

FILOMENA

Pampinea, stop being so lame! Like we're not fucking nuns,
Also last time I checked none of us got med degrees?
Like all of us are scared of blood anyway
and we're the weaker sex.

EMILIA

Ew blood is so scary.

PAMPINEA

Ya blood does suck.

FILOMENA

You should just enjoy being here,
like everything is so green
and all the butterflies sing to us
and we're all so young and hot, like especially Emilia.

EMILIA

I really am, thanks Filomens ;)

LAURETTA

Get itttt

FILOMENA

Like this could be the best moment of our livesss,
Like here, now, away from everyone holding us back,
Like dying and stuff.

EMILIA

Ya, you're so right. It's good we all can afford to do this.
Everyone needs to leave town from time to time.

LAURETTA

Ya, and it's nice to be missed,
Like I'm sure all the rabid birds and cats
Near ma house miss me a lot
And that means sooo much.

PAMPINEA

Well maybe Filomena, THIS is the best time of YOUR life,
Cause you have a bf who loves you
And is good looking enough to be socially acceptable
but all I have is female friendship
Which is not erotic enough for me.

EMILIA

Oh come on, Pampinea.
I've seen you talk with Dioneo??
Sure he likes you.

PAMPINEA

Ugh, no he likes you cause you're hotter than me.

EMILIA

…oops

FILOMENA

Ugh you guys are boring me and saying nothing,
let's just get our patron saint, Clarita,
the patron saint of sewing and smiling,
to come down and give us some advice.

LADIES

Kk cool.

(CLARITA comes down from heaven.)

CLARITA

Good day fair ladies,
I'm the patron saint of sewing and smiling,
How can I be of service to you?

FILOMENA

Pampinea has a crush and we have like
No clue
What he's thinking.

CLARITA

Well does he smile at you?

PAMPINEA

I don't think so…no.

FILOMENA

Oh wait! Once I think I saw him smile at her…but it might
Have been at the two squirrels biting each other
Behind her…
He has kinda a twisted mind.

EMILIA

Yaaa totally

CLARITA

That all sounds weird.
Why do you even like this boy Pampinea?
My son is actually single…
He wrestles and stuff and has a 6 pack
I can introduce you.

PAMPINEA

Uhh that's ok. I dunno why I like him, he's just like so
Free..to say whatever,
Be whatever.
I wish I could be that free, ya feel me Clarita?

CLARITA

I actually do. But he sounds slightly unstable
Maybe you should try to squelch your desire,
But if you can't, just sew his face on something
And sit near him while you sew it
And smile hard at him the whole time you sew,
Men love-that. Clarita, out!

(CLARITA disappears.)

PAMPINEA

Hmmmm

LAURETTA

That was kinda weird advice.

FILOMENA

Whatevers, it was fine.

EMILIA

Her son sounded kinda hot though.

FILOMENA

Keep it in your pants Emilia.

EMILIA

Kkkk sorry.

(Men come back and everyone is sitting.)

FILOMENA

Oh, who desires to tell a story
On the third day!
Who has something to share?

DIONEO

I'm not ready yet…

PAMPINEA

I shall go!

(Ladies and Gents sit.)

PAMPINEA

So this story is about a man who would go to any
Length to prove his wife was worthy
Of him.
A man who treated a woman so badly
Some would call child protective services.
It's kinda like Cinderella…but more depressing.
So it all starts when Gaultiere, the king,
Was getting pressure from his noblemen to marry.
I shall play the tortured wife!
Filomena and Lauretta will you play nobleman 1 and 2??
And um Dioneo…
I think you'd be great for Gaultiere!

DIONEO

Score!

*(PAMPINEA gives a script to FILOMENA,
LAURETTA and DIONEO.)*

LAURETTA (as NOBLEMAN 2)
We've been thinking about something important
Gaultiere and we need to share,
you need an heir Gaultiere
Like how is our town supposed to live on?

DIONEO (as GAULTIERE)
But I'm fine just hunting and sleeping and doing me
Alsooo
What if I get someone spoiled?
Like so fucking spoiled and awful and hot,
And she like asks me to talk to her
On the phone for hours every night
And wants me to remember facts about
Her childhood?
Like that's literally upsetting to me.

LAURETTA (as NOBLEMAN 2)
Don't worry so much,
Not like we're gunna pick someone for you.
You can pick someone of your own choosing!
Andddd
You can find someone better than that fictional chick,
Of course you can!!

FILOMENA (as NOBLEMAN 1)
My wife has legit social anxiety, and never speaks,
It's so hot! Maybe she has a cousin, I can look…

DIONEO (as GAULTIERE)
Hmm I guess…
Well actually one fair lass springs to mind's eye,
There's this poor chick who lives close to the castle,
A fair wench. I saw her milk a cow once

DIONEO (as GAULTIERE, cont))
While I was having my morning tea
Made of gold,
And she milked it so slowly
I almost had to go to the hospital because
Of all the feelings it stirred,
It was quite upsetting at the time,
Like I couldn't even feel my body.

FILOMENA (as NOBLEMAN 1)
That sounds like love sir!

LAURETTA (as NOBLEMAN 2)
Peasants are so
hot.
They are also so
Sad. I don't know why I find sad women hotter...
They just are.
Life is so mysterious.

FILOMENA (as NOBLEMAN 1)
Totally.

DIONEO (as GAULTIERE)
Well it is decreed, I shall marry...her

FILOMENA (as NOBLEMAN 1)
Wait, what is her name?

DIONEO (as GAULTIERE)
Shh! I am talking!
I will marry the fair peasant, name TBD
And she shall be my wife and do well by me
And make me breakfast from scratch
And milk my cows slowly and
Take care of me both in and out of the bedroom.

FILOMENA (as NOBLEMAN 1)
That was a really really romantic speech.
Have you thought about writing a book?
Cause I know a guy….

DIONEO (as GAULTIERE)
And so I chose the fair peasant woman for my wife
And bought her from her father, v affordable,
And she was brought to the castle for marriage and merriment,
And all of the noblemen were so into her as a future leader
And she laughed at their jokes
So well.
And everything seemed to be perfect:

(GRISELDA and GAULTIERE address the audience.)

PAMPINEA (as GRISELDA)
I'm like so lucky
To be here and he has the best hands,
Like not like a farmer's hands that feel
Like sandpaper and broken dreams, and he chose me!
Like little old me,
Out of all the milkmaids in all the land.

DIONEO (as GAULTIERE)
It's weird, I thought I'd never be married,
I thought I could spend the rest of ma days
Egging children and stealing people's
Tax money,
And going on medieval bar crawls, but everything's different now.
And she seems so nice, like she seems like
lemon butter or falling stars,
but like should I have done this?

PAMPINEA (as GRISELDA)

I wonder if he's thinking about me,
Like how my cheeks will feel if he touches me,
If they'll blossom like a million
High class
Roses, or if they'll just feel like
Cheeks.
(I hope they'll feel better than that.)
We talk and talk and each word he says sounds prettier
And prettier, and I hardly ever have to
Milk a cow again or hang with a goat,
I can just like get my nails done and chill

DIONEO (as GAULTIERE)

Like am I even the marrying kind? Cause I just feel like
How am I supposed to trust a member of the fairer sex?
Like how do I know she won't run off with a rando
Hot dude who kinda looks like me?
And I don't even like her that much anyway
Cause she kinda looks like
My cousin from a weird angle,
But maybe that's ok.
And suddenly I feel this bubbling feeling
Growing within me: I just wanna…
I want her to feel so baddd,
Like sit on your kitchen floor
Eating-Entenmann-donuts-and-crying-into-them bad
Like I just wanna
Haze her, like I wanna see her heart break like 100 times
Like in slow motion
Like at meee, like preferably naked,
like I want her to
Never think another man exists besides me,
Like need me so much she can't remember how to breath
Like I just have to help her live
Cause she just can't do anything anymore,
Like she'll just be fricking lostttt!!

PAMPINEA (as GRISELDA)

So years go by and I have this baby girl whose as
Cute as a teacup pig
And I feel like..fulfilled or something,
But then one day he takes her from me,
To an early death and he asks me how I feel about that
And I smile and smile
And say I'm fine
And I let my mind go blank
And try to think about nothing
And I remember that once I did have nothing
Except a father with bad teeth
And a goat that kicked me in the face while
I was in the bathroom,
I had nothinggg and now I have everything,
And aren't I lucky?
I guess I have everything I ever wanted
So it would be selfish to not be grateful as fuck.
And then some years pass by and he turns to me and
Says "Your beauty is gone,
You're too old to be hot now,I shall replace you"
And my insides explode like a volcano going through
menopause
But I remember
I used to sleep in a farm shed the size of NY studio
And I used to only talk to beetles
And goats and I have a new life now,
And maybe if I pretend like
I don't feel things he'll take me back,
And from far away sometimes he looks like a sexy glass
horse.
So he strips me and takes me back to the farm
And it's like nothing ever changed, like
The whole fairytale is this weird hangover dream
And my dad's eyes tell me "told you so"
And I feel those syllables course throughout my body

PAMPINEA (as GRISELDA, cont)

And almost strangle me.
But I smile and breath
And resume my old life,
And I scoop and I milk and I churn
And I feel invisible.
And on really really cold nights where we do karaoke
With the goats
I would think about him
And how he smelled like manly lilacs and
How he smiled at me so wide like so surprised
That I put up with him,
And I just miss him so bad, so bad it
gnaws at me and then one day he shows up.

DIONEO (as GAULTIERE)

And I tell her that our children are alive
And fine and that I lied
To test her.
And I ask her to be mine again and in a second
She agrees.
And we eat overpriced five foot tall cake
Shaped like a big heart
That's filled-with edible semi-alchoholic confetti

PAMPINEA (as GRISELDA)

And we're back together and I'm happy
I think.
So happy I can't feel my body,
like the kind of happy you
get from being on a radical diet then
eating a whole box of donuts
within two minutes
and you feel like you might pass out
or also throw up,
but it was worth it.

DIONEO (as GAULTIERE)
And we rejoice, and everything makes sense again
And I don't tell her
How good her suffering made me feel,
how I could feel it in everyone of my bones
and I might do this again in another year
cause like monogamy be boring...
you gotta spice it up
you know how it is?

(GRISELDA and GAULTIERE makeout.)

DIONEO
Hmm that was kinda depressing...

LAURETTA
But kinda romantic!

EMILIA
Like she deserves way better,
Like someone who doesn't steal
Her children...
Like someone who cooks her
Butterscotch cupcakes every morning
Like someone who sews her undergarments
With hearts on them
With zest.

(transition: Dioneo and Emilia.)

DIONEO
Hey, I like that daisy in your hair.

EMILIA
Thankssssss, flowers rock!

DIONEO

How's it going? You enjoying the stories
And stuff?

EMILIA

Oh yaa, I love stories
Like so fun to listen to and stuff
Like so many twists and turns
Like so engrossing and stuff like they always get me

DIONEO

Ya, totally…you know I notice you?
Like when no one's watching,
like sometimes your hair looks a little orange
in the sunlight
and sometimes your laugh sounds like a sweet chuckle
and other times like a 90-year-old farmer dude's
like "hohoho" and you smile so wide like all the time
and I like that and do you notice thingss about me?

EMILIA

Ummmms
You're always really clean?
Like you seem to bathe a lot…
I respect THAT! Good for U!
I come from a long line of serious bathers
We all smell really good
Like lilacs and good values,
So I really do respect that and stuff.

DIONEO

What do you care about? What keeps you up at night? If you
could be any kind of turnip, which turnip would it be?

EMILIA

One: I care about true love and saving
Baby animals and making sure all ma friends
Like me at all times.
Two: Um I guess like whatever like we're all gunna die from
the plague
So that's scary
And also, I like thinking about mint chocolate chip
Ice cream and what it feels like in ma mouth
And how cold and comforting it is on ma tongue

DIONEO

Wowwwwwww ;)

EMILIA

And finally, ma fave kind of turtles
Are baby turtles cause they just are so innocent
And like see everythin' anew,
Like everything is a surprise to them.

DIONEO

That's really cool.
You know sometimes I miss being home,
I miss it so bad it hurts,
Cause there were so many feral cats near my home
I'd tell stories to,
And so many commoners to throw rocks at,
And just so much stuff going on,
But then I think it's ok,
Cause I'm here, and you're here
And no one's going anywhere and
That's perfect and
I think I could care about you.

EMILIA

Woahhhh…
Um
Wow,
I mean uhhh
Thanks?
Kkkk cool.

DIONEO

Do you reciprocate my feelings?

EMILIA

I have to...
Pee....

(EMILIA runs away.)

Day 4- It's getting hot in hereeeee

(PANFILO is smoking weed. FILOMENA is annoyed by him. The whole company is onstage either playing cards or sewing, looking kinda like an old painting like serene. They don't listen to FILOMENA's and PANFILO's conversation.)

PANFILO

You chew kinda weird sometimes you know that?

FILOMENA

Not really…
Like I did like a bazillion etiquette
Seminars wit ma mom so…
Like I'm a woman, like of course etiquette is a top priority

PANFILO

No it's not bad man, just noticed ittt
Like woahhh
Like your mouth just gets sooo widdddeeee??
Ugh is it weird I've been feeling
Like really itchy lately,
And like
Part of my left leg
Has turned a light shade of green?

FILOMENA

I'm sure not, probs stress,
You should meditate more?

PANFILO

Kkkk

FILOMENA

Ugh but can we like focussss????
Dating is hard sometimes you know??
Like we've been dating like 100 days and stuff and
Most of my friends get married after like
10 days and stuff and it's just like I
Know I shouldn't compare,
Buttt like it's hard not to cause they walk
All over town
Like showing off their new bling and their betrothed
Just looks so into them
And babies try to grope their new bauble in glee
And animals run behind them
And for some reason the sun just likes them better
And just seems to capture them in the best light ever
And is it bad I want that?

PANFILO

Comparing yourself is fruitless, Filomena!
Like maybe cause I come from a more low key part
Of Italy, I don't do that,
Ugh this convo would be way better wit Cheetos though,
I kinda wanna watch you chew,
Like it legittt entertains me,
So you should feel good about that!

FILOMENA

I guess I just thought that after 60 days or so
it would happen
or after 70 days, but it just has not,
and maybe I'm basic for expecting something,
but is it wrong to want things to happen fast?
Like I want to be so special
Someone doesn't know what to do with meee
Like I'm dangerous to them in a hot way,
Like act fast or I'll explode,

PANFILO

It's just a really big step ok…
Honey bear face
I just need to work more at selling and buying things
And get my finances in order,
I'm still young-ish,
It's not really about you, like I'm not thinking about you at
all,
Just about me
And money and I love Cheetos.
So don't worry about anything ok!
Look at those branches over there,
So brown and fragile,
They blow ever so lightly with the wind,
The earth is so beautiful, so filled with God's creations,
Focus on that baby sour patch kid,
Focus on the world,

PANFILO (cont)

Like plus we'll probs all die soon anyway
Like so soon and then our bodies
Will become pink and yellow
And green and float into the ethers
And woahhhhhhh freakyyyyy

FILOMENA

kkkkkkk
Sorry for worrying.
Most of our relatives have prob died by now anyway,
So it's probs a moot point,
Like probs doesn't matter.

(back to group.)

LAURETTA

Hey guys,
I think my story is gunna be different,
I wrote a little song for you guys,
So feel free to dance and stuff!

*(During LAURETTA's song the ladies and gents
dance, as the song escalates the vibing between
everyone escalates till it gets sexi.)*

There once was a girl named Nistrato,
And she dreamed of true love,
But in the meantime, she made her pets hook up
And get married and stuff
Cause that was close enough for now
She was lonely,
But when she turned at the hot age of 16
She met someone
With hair as fine as gold,
Like if she was poor she could have cut off his hair

And sold it for something,
But that would have been creepy since she didn't know him,
Also she was supa rich, she bathed in dolla bills
The man's name was Jupiter, said her personality was bangin
And they would sit all day together
Talking about nothing
And Nistrato waited for him to make "the move"
She waited for years, waited and waited
And then one day a woman walked by
Who had won a swimsuit competition
And Jupiter left and followed her
And no moves were made
No moves were made
No moves were made
She wanted some moves and no moves were made
And then soon after received a wedding invite
To the wedding of Jupiter and the swimsuit chick
And she attended and watched the whole thing
And at night while they were in
Their fantasy suite
She crawled in through the window while they were sleeping
And she cut off all his hair
And she used it to make a baby wig for her pet frog
And then she made a little frog wedding
And after that she disappeared into a swamp
Never to be heard from again,
She thought being in love was enough, but it wasn't, it
wasn't
She wasn't enough, she wasn't she wasn't,
She wasn't good enough for a hetero mannnnn,
But maybe she would be enough for a man of the sea,
Like a merman?? Is that what you call it? The swamp had a
lot
The enddddd

(Everyone claps for LAURETTA.)

PANFILO

What a tune!
Could you make me a CD?

LAURETTA

Totes! Ya I would be honored.
What did you think Filostrato?
I can make you a CD also, or like 20…

FILOSTRATO (to FILOMENA)

Wow, you're a really good dancer.

FILOMENA

Thankssss.

EMILIA

It's like I can finally feel my body

PAMPINEA

I see that…

DIONEO

Mhhhhhhmmmmm

PANFILO

It's like we're free or something
Like I'm a bird or something
And just can fly wherever I wanttt,
Like go anywhere.
Wait babes, what are you doing??

FILOMENA

Umm nothing….

FILOSTRATO

:

Day 5- It's getting even hotter in here

(Ladies on one side and gentleman on the other.)

LAURETTA

What does it feel like?
To likeee
Do the act?
To be so sinful…
I can't imagine…

PAMPINEA

OMG Me neither.

FILOMENA

I want to imagine but I cannot!

EMILIA

It's no bigs really
Like it hurts a little at firsttt
Like someone's trying to pull your hair out slowly
But with time it eases up
And it starts to feel like someone throwing candy at you,
Which is painful but also I like candy!
I luvvv candyyy

PAMPINEA

Who did you even do it wit??

FILOMENA

Your so sluttttiii,
No one does it before they're marrieddd,
Like how did it even happennnn??

EMILIA

It was no bigsss,
I just like hooked up wit my baby sitter a few times
Like wen I was 16 or whatevss,
He was like too hot to be a babysitter,
calm it downnn.

PAMPINEA

Will anyone want to marry you thoooough??
Like that is your precious gift
And a babysitter stole it away!
Just saying it out loud is even more upsetting.

EMILIA

I'm sure a guy…or someone
will still like me or whatevss

FILOMENA

Just don't tell them
And I'm sure it'll be fine.
When I am married to Panfilo,
We will commit the act and what
Beauty shall be had!

LAURETTA

Was he like ummm
Good at it?

EMILIA

Ya it was fine,
Like no bigs
Like at the beginning he was kinda quiet and shit
But then I like smacked him a lot during it
And I think it upset him so he started
Sucking lesss.

LAURETTA/FILOMENA/PAMPINEA (saying different
lines)
I'm waiting till marriage
Who would ever want me?
Your babysitter sounds hot
I fucking hate myself

(Focus on the group of men.)

FILOSTRATO
What is it like, to get to date
Filomena?
She makes even the hottest ladies look like a garbage
Bag.

PANFILO
Like so nice and pleasant!
We make out so much and stuff like
Cause we can't do anything else
Till we're married and it's good,
Except sometimes she can get a little violent while we
makeout
During it and says things like
"Marry me now or I'll fucking kill you"
Which upsets me for a moment, but it's no bigs really.

DIONEO
I once was with a chick who tried to
Stick her father's dagger in me
Duringgg it,
I almost died but it was so fricking erotic, I can't
#worthit
Who doesn't like a chick with zest in the bedroom?

FILOSTRATO

Oh what jealousy fills ma bod!!
I wish I had done it, but alas all my exes were awful…
And wanted to wait till we were betrothed.

PANFILO

Ya supa jealussss
Speaking of adventurous chicks,
I think Lauretta likes you Filostrato…

DIONEO

Oh ya she is so into dat.

FILOSTRATO

Huh? What makes you say that?

PANFILO

She wrote a song called "I'm madly in love with you
Filostrato, take my body, I burn for you in the even"

FILOSTRATO

So what?
You're being supa literal right now
Like art is meant to provoke and shit,
like wet the taste buds, like justt
cause my name is in her song doesn't mean anything.

DIONEO

Well what do you think of her?
I find her body
to be hot.

FILOSTRATO

Uhhhhhhhhhrrrr
Welllll

(focus on the girls.)

58

PAMPINEA

Filomenaaa,
There's something weird I noticed…but like I can't tell
If it's just me…

FILOMENA

Whattt?

PAMPINEA

Filostrato like looks at you like ALL
The time
Like stares at you
All the time
Like what's the deal with that??

FILOMENA

That's odd,
I noticed no such thing

PAMPINEA

I once saw him making out with a scroll with a hand
Drawn pic of your face on it.

EMILIA

I once saw him make a shrine for you
And live outside it for one full year.

PAMPINEA

I once saw him almost jump off a cliff and he was shouting
your name!

FILOMENA

Well why didn't you stop him??

LAURETTA

This convo is sooo upsetting to meee,
Raaaaa, I don't think I can live anymore.

EMILIA

I dunno…I like to observe human life
And not like make changes to it

FILOMENA

Well I don't care what you say about Filostrato
My heart belongs to Panfilo,
And he can do with it as he will!

PAMPINEA

Omg you two so cute #couplegoals #icanteven #sosingle
#IloveDioneosomuchkillme

LAURETTA

You two are seriousllly so cute,
Like I'm writing a song about you two!
Like you two are so cute and such a great couplllle
Like it legit makes me weepy
Ug I want a boyfrienddd
Ug I love Filostrato so much,
Glad he didn't jump off a cliff,
His anger towards his exes is so hot to meee.

EMILIA

Well if you likeee him so much, you should tell him.

FILOMENA

Great idea, not!
Ladies don't tell men their feelings,
Not at all proper.
Like read ma etiquette blog.

LAURETTA

It's true! I just feel like he would freak if I told himmm,
Like it would just change the world order,
Like the sun will stop beaming,
And the rain will dry up and it's just not naturalll!!!??

FILOMENA

Woah, calm it down.
(Think you just spit on me???)

EMILIA

What if it doesn't even matter?
Like none of you guys will even do it
Cause like we're gunna get sick man,
Like we can't help it
And then we'll never get nice weddings
And wear dresses too expensive to look at,
Like what if that happpensss?

(Focus on the guys.)

FILOSTRATO

Like she seems ok I guess, I dunno.
I barely notice her,
Like she has bad hair,
Like also she seems so angsty all the time,
Like I didn't know chicks could be that angsty,
Like she's kinda as attractive to me as a mop,
But like I don't think about it that much,
Like her that much.

DIONEO

I think Pampinea is into me…
She keeps looking at me and licking her lips
Or something?
Not sure if it's on purpose or like a tick?
But being with her would be like dating Bambi,

DIONEO (cont)

Like she's so fucking nice all the timeee
Like women should be nice, but that's like too niceee.

PANFILO

Don't worry about her,
I still think you should go for Emilia.
She is very attractive to me
And spaces out in the best moments,
Classic hilarityyyy!

DIONEO

I wonder what she would look like naked…
Probably good.

FILOMENA

I saw it once, ya know?
Nothing happened but
It looks like the moon I guess,
Like silver and effervescent
And you're scared to touch it
And you don't have to, until he wants to have a life wit you,
You just stare at it.

PANFILO

Filomena's body feels like the earth,
Like so natural and easy to touch
Like she makes me feel like a sexy farmer, like a late-night
farmer
Like weeding and plucking her,
But nothing that interesting happened,
Since we are not betrothed yet.

DIONEO

What a great metaphor.

LAURETTA

I enjoyed that metaphor!
Oh, will someone tell a story!?
This talk is making me blush and a lady
Cannot blush all the day long,
Oh distract us, distract us!

FILOMENA

I actually have a good one, men gather round!
Panfy, will you act??

PANFILO

Of course!
I thought my earlier part in Filostrato's
Was way too small,
So excited for another chance in the spotlight!

(FILOMENA gives PANFILO a script.)

FILOMENA

So like I have a story about true love gone wrong,
Life can be hard, I suggest you all
Huddle close with your friends,
Take out your medieval scotch and listen to the tale of
Puppeta and
Marvin.
So Puppeta was a beautiful young lass,
But not just normal beautiful,
Like the kinda beauty that inspires wars and
Twitter fights,
I shall play her, of course.

FILOMENA (as PUPPETA)

Ever since I was young I dreamed of my perfect
Wedding
I dreamed of the dress I would wear,
It would be covered in pearls

FILOMENA (as PUPPETA, cont)
And have mermaid tail sequins all over it
And there would be just the right amount of cleavage
And I imagined everyone in my family in
In awe of me
And my decision to be hetero and marry a dude.
It would be so romantic!!
And all of my servants would serenade
me with an insanely romantic song
That would be so romantic peeps would pass out
And one of my servants would be recruited
For Medieval
American Idol
And all of my single friends would
Be heartbroken and so jealous
They could eat it and
They would realize at that moment,
That the wedding was too perfect and they couldn't top it
So they all died alone and remained spinsters
And had lots of guinea pigs as life partners,
I would imagine this over and over
But then one day I met someone,
A real man!

PANFILO (as MARVIN)
Greetings Fair lady, my name is Marvin.

FILOMENA (as PUPPETA)
They call me Puppeta.

PANFILO (as MARVIN)
Your name sounds like "puppet."
I enjoyed when my father played with puppets
For me
As a child,
So I'm into that,
Like your name I mean.

FILOMENA (as PUPPETA)

And we dated for 6 long months
Longer than any other lass courted before being betrothed
And then one day
I couldn't bare it anymore
And threw away my feminine modesty
And asked about....
Their FUTURE!
"Oh sweet pure hearted Marvin,
We have spent time with each other for
6 long months,
Longer than any other lass in the HISTORY of time
Has spent time with a man while not being betrothed,
Like I love going to the caves with you
To scare bears but is there anything else
You might want to do with me??"

PANFILO (as MARVIN)

Not really...
Like I like you so much Puppeta,
You are so attractive to the eye
But I am happy as we are.

FILOMENA (as PUPPETA)

But do you ever think about marriage?
Like do you think about what kinda wedding dress I would
wear
How it would be glow in the darkkk
Or be waterproof so I could swim in it
And also sad jealous chicks could cry on me
Like don't you want commoners to
Look on us!
Like with so much awe, case we experienced
The truest of love
And want to shout it from the hilltops!

PANFILO (as MARVIN)
Nope, don't really
Ponder such matters.

FILOMENA (as PUPPETA)
Ugh
But no one else in our time period
Waits this long for marriagggge,
My bff Vanilla got betrothed after a week of dating a rando
sailor

PANFILO (as MARVIN)
But we aren't Vanilla, we are us…

FILOMENA (as PUPPETA)
But what if I want to be Vanilla and a rando sailor!

PANFILO (as MARVIN)
But we are not them!

FILOMENA (as PUPPETA)
I need to use the restroom.
And in that moment, I knew.
I knew that my dream celebration
Was but a flight of fancy and fated to never come true
And Marvin loved me in a chill kinda way
Like the kinda love you have for Gatorade
Or a goldfish,
And not the kinda way that burns forests
Or changes people's lives
And so I went to the restroom
And took a golden knife from her bosom
And proceeded to cut out my heart
And I walked back into the room
And gave it to Marvin as a present,
And then proceeded to die as he watched
Note- I died very slowly.

FILOMENA (as PUPPETA, cont)

The end!!

PANFILO

Woahhhh! So dramatic! What a story Babe!

EVERYONE ELSE

....

(EMILIA and PAMPINEA are sewing.)

EMILIA

This blankets gunna look so good!

PAMPINEA

Who is it for?

EMILIA

My sister just had a baby
Named Martinus
And I want to sew him a blanket!
Like a cute blanket, like a welcome to the world kinda
blanket.

PAMPINEA

Kewll

EMILIA

What are you working on?

PAMPINEA

You talk a lot while you work,
Don't you?

EMILIA

Sorrryyy…
It like relaxes me..
Like helps get me in the mood…
To sew.

PAMPINEA

If you must know,
I'm working on a hat for Filomena
Cause like we succcch good friends
And like our friendship is so important to meee
And I'm just like so luckkky to have her
In ma life
#blessed.
She also has great hair and needs a hat that like respects that,
Like respects her face shape.

EMILIA

She does have really good hair…
Um I'm sorry Dioneo likes me or whatever,
Like I don't likeee him at all though so…

PAMPINEA

I don't hate you at all
Like women don't experience hate
Cause we are made up of rainbow butterflies
And candy canes and purity mashed up
Together like a smoothie
And COURSE I don't hate you.

EMILIA

I didn't suggest you hated me…

PAMPINEA

It's just Dioneo is just like so himself,
And has such a healthy sex drive!
Like not scared to talk about that,
Like no sense of modesty, ug so hottt

EMILIA

I think Dioneo is an idiot
Not to notice you.
You are so much nicer than everyone else,
And you have this openness about you
Like so open like you're a fricking door,
Like an open door, but in a cute way

PAMPINEA

Oh :)

EMILIA

I think your hats gunna be very fashion forward

PAMPINEA

Thanks :)
Srry I was so mean to you,
Guess I just thought you liked him also,
Like how passionate he gets when he says we should all play
Naked poker,
Like it's beautiful
Like so hopeful
Getting me a little riled up just thinking about it

EMILIA

I can see that.

PAMPINEA

Do you um care for anyone like that?

EMILIA

I guess there's someone
But it's kinda stupid
Like others would think it was stupid
And also maybe punishable by death :/ (oops!)

PAMPINEA

Oh do you like Panfilo or something?
Cause you're right,
I do think Filomena would kill you?
He's a bit too nice and stonery for my taste…

(EMILIA grabs PAMPINEA and kisses her.)

What just happened?

EMILIA

I dunno! Fuck!
I wasn't supposed to do that!
But I guess um
The world's ending soon and all I can think about
Is your eyes
They pierce me
And also sometimes you whip out this great smize
Like you must be an America's Next top model fan or
something
also that face shape is not one of nature,
Say something??
Like couldn't you tell I like you
Like cause of that story and stuff I told
Like about secret lovas…

PAMPINEA

I thought it was just like a story.

EMILIA

Well it wasn't,
It possessed the subtext.
And there wasn't even a "stage kiss"
In the story, I just like
Wrote it in.
Can I kiss you again?

PAMPINEA

Ya

(They kiss.)

PAMPINEA

I don't know what I'm doing
I thought I hated you…
But maybe hate is a hotter emotion than I realized
(I don't know what I'm doing!!!)

EMILIA

I don't know what I'm doing either
I don't think anyone does

PAMPINEA

Let's just like um
Never tell anyone this ever happened ever
(Cause like proper ladies shouldn't do this
And Filomena would kill me)
But like maybe keep doing it
Like forever and ever???

EMILIA

Ya into it.

(They makeout. Shift to group of guys and gals.)

DIONEO

Ugh I feel like today has gone on so long,
It's been an entire month.

PAMPINEA

It's weird like I feel fine, ya know?
And then I have this intense flashback
Of like everyone I know dying slowly...
And then I get sad again,
I don't get it...

FILOSTRATO

It's ok Pampinea,
Just try to think less....

FILOMENA

Ugh this garden is almost becoming too attractive
And it's annoying me,
I miss ma extra-large Barbie themed water bed :(

PANFILO

You'll see it again baberellaa!
At least I hope so....

LAURETTA

Oh cheer up sweet friends!
I know something that should be celebratedddd?!?
That will cheer everyone up!!
(Who said that!?) (What's she talking abouttt?!

PANFILO

Erkkkk

> *(Note on LAURETTA's announcement- there's
> something kinda kids "birthday party" about it/
> bad prom-posal.)*

LAURETTA

I have an announcement to make!
I know women should not express their feelings ever
And I do apologize to my patron saint Clarita for this
announcement
But I need to share it or my heart will burst
Into a million pop rocks or doves or
Pieces of bacon and I can't hold it any longerrr-
I have fallen
For a member of the male sex...
He is in this room???
His name is Filostrato and he is sitting right there.

DIONEO (to Filostrato)

That's you man!

LAURETTA

Filostrato, will you come over here???

FILOSTRATO

Uhhh....ok.

DIONEO

Do it man! Maybe she'll give you cake!
I love cake!

FILOMENA

(OMG this is so embarrassing
I dunno if I can ever talk to you againnn)

LAURETTA

Do you care for me as a woman??
Please be honest, I want to know your heart,
I want to read it fast and true like
A relly good beach read aimed at women.

FILOSTRATO

Ummm
I'm good?

LAURETTA

Well yes, I find that to be true as well.
You are a good man!
I agree

FILOSTRATO

I just mean um…like I'm good not being with you…
Like I don't like you like that…
Like your music is too emo for my liking
And your face isn't cute enuf for my liking
And
Fuck everyone's looking at me

LAURETTA

ya….
Well thanks for telling me.

FILOSTRATO

Your welcome.
I guess it's good for you to know right.

(LAURETTA starts crying. FILOSTRATO starts dancing cause he doesn't know what else to do.)

Day 6- Let's stop being polite, let's start gettin Reallll

DIONEO

Ok so this story is hot
So I apologize in advanced
If it upsets the ladies,
But at the same time,
I don't care
And don't really apologize.

DIONEO (cont)
So this story is about this young, supa hot young lass named
Alibech,
Emlia…you can play that part.

(DIONEO gives script to EMILIA.)

EMILIA
Actually, I'm good.

(EMILIA goes and sits next to PAMPINEA.)

LAURETTA
I can read!
I've been wanting to expand
From a single threat to a double threat,
Like acting and singing.

DIONEO
That's fine.
Here's the script.

(DIONEO gives the script to LAURETTA.)

LAURETTA (as ALIBECH)
All I ever wanted since I was young was to serve God,
I couldn't sew or milk cows or do anything useful,
But I did love God a lot.
I always had so many questions for God:
Like what was his fave color?
Did he like roller blading or ice skating more?
To interject: I assume it is roller blading,
So one day I realized my
Plain life as a maiden wasn't good enough anymore
And I had to find a better way to serve God,
So I left my plain life

LAURETTA (as ALIBECH, cont)
And started on the hunt for a new home,
Which was not as easy a search as I thought it would be.
And over and over I thought:
"Oh, all I want is to serve God
But I go to house after house and am rejected.
They say I am too young and hot to be in a rando man's
home
And that is UPSETTING
to
Me!
What does wanting to serve God
And hotness have to do with each other?
I think nothing!"
But finally I find a house,
The home of Rustico the noble monk,

DIONEO (as RUSTICO)
And when I meet her, I am not scared of her
Intense, overwhelming hotness,
Since I am a man of God himself.
But at the same time…
I am still a man, ya feel meeee??

LAURETTA (as ALIBECH)
And I meet him and I say,
Oh please, help me serve God!
I think about him all the time! Like I can't stop!
Can't stop won't stop
All I want is to help him
And help transform this fine earth
Into a better and more noble place for all.

DIONEO (as Rustico)

Sounds like a good cause.
You are so hot, I mean um sorry,
Welcome to my home!
Stay away from me! I mean um,
Go read that Bible over there!

LAURETTA (as ALIBECH)

Certainly!
I love the Bible!

DIONEO (as RUSTICO)

So she reads the Bible
Day in and day out, and I
Taught her many lessons about
The characters in the great story,
But then one day I had another kind of lesson for her,
And I say to her
"I will now get undressed."

LAURETTA (as ALIBECH)

Why?
I do not understand.

DIONEO (as Rustico)

Um
Sacred cleaning of the body
You are way more committed to God that way
When…naked.

LAURETTA (as ALIBECH)

Then I'll do it too! Woot!

DIONEO (as Rustico)
(points to his lower regionsss)
Do you see this body part I have?
It is very bad and upsetting to me, it is the Devil.
The Devil is on ma bod and I need help.

LAURETTA (as ALIBECH)
But how can I help you?
Oo shall we cut it off?
I have some garden shears in my bedroom!

DIONEO (as Rustico)
Oh no!
No um that idea displeases me!
No, I must learn to live, to deal with the Devil,
Man will always have to deal with his sin,
But there is a way you can help,
Do you see that part of you between your legs,
That is hell.

LAURETTA (as ALIBECH)
What an awful day, to learn that both of us
Are stricken with such
Negative things on our bodies
That people spend their whole lives dreading,
I pity us both.

DIONEO (as RUSTICO)
Oh but do not be distressed sweet Alibech,
For if I lie on top of you
I can return the devil to hell.

LAURETTA (as ALIBECH)
Oh wow! I'd love to put the devil back in hell!
For so long I've wanted to do something important,
To really do Gods work
And finally I can!

DIONEO (as RUSTICO)
And so they put the devil back in hell
Multiple times!
That devil really hung out in hell a lot,
But after a few weeks Rustico
Felt his age and tired of Alibech and her need to do Gods
work.

LAURETTA (as ALIBECH)
Why do we never put the devil back in hell anymore??
If I want to one day be a nun,
I must do Gods work at least 3 times a day!
And also it's fun!

DIONEO (as RUSTICO)
Oh Alibech,
You are young and I have a dad bod
And am woefully out of shape,
I cannot do Gods work the way someone so young can.

LAURETTA (as ALIBECH)
Well I want to put the devil back in hell!
The devil is awful and needs to go back to his home!
So unfairrr

DIONEO (as RUSTICO)
Well you're a woman,
Many things are unfair and will be that way for centuries!
You must make do with putting the devil back in hell
Four times a week.

LAURETTA (as ALIBECH)
15!

DIONEO (as RUSTICO)
3.

LAURETTA (as ALIBECH)

"You can suck it,
You are so disrespectful to the Lord!
Lets makeout!"
So for many nights and days I fought with Rustico.
I felt like he was hurting my chances
Of helping God
And I love loveee helping God.
But then one-day I got word
That my father and all my relatives have died intensely
In my family home
In an intense fire
and that a young man
Named Tutum was looking for me
To help sort out my finances.
Soon Tutum shows up at Rustico's home
And he just seems so boring
And all he likes talking about is
How pears are an underrated fruit
And did I agree? And if not, then I suck
And it's like my whole fricking family died brah,
Like I'm not in the mood for fruit debate,
But he takes me back to his home
And all I can do is cry,
I cry so much a river grows
Around Rustico's house, the sexiest
And saddest river that ever happened.
When you touch the river you start crying
And your top comes off.

DIONEO (as RUSTICO)

And she leaves and I am
secretly relieved since
It was getting to be a lot of effort
And ma dad bod relly couldn't handle it.
And soon I get notice that Tutum and Alibech

DIONEO (as RUSTICO, cont)
Are to be married and I of course
attends their wedding
And it was rocking
and loved my celebratory t-shirt
I got in the gift bag.

LAURETTA (as ALIBECH)
And on the wedding night, Tutum comes near me
And proceeds to touch me
Like Rustico touched me
And to my delight I realized
We did have something in common,
We both cared about doing God's work.
And we lived happily ever after!
The end!

(All the women pass out. The men don't know what to do.)

FILOSTRATO
That was a pretty cool story Dioneo.
I hope to put the devil back in hell one day
Too!

DIONEO
Yasss get ittt!

FILOMENA
I need some sunnnnnnn!!

LADIES (at different times)
Yassss!
I need some sunnnnn.
I wanna be so tan I look like a tree

(Shift- Even later that day. Ladies all sitting together. They are a little turned on by thinking of DIONEO's story, but pretend to be offended… they suck at pretending. *Note: In this scene EMILIA and PAMPINEA are hardcore vibing but trying to not show it.)

FILOMENA
God, these guys are so gross!!
Ackkk!
Like so gross. Like I'm
so
offended I can't even deal.
Like who even thinks of such stories?

PAMPINEA
Yaaa, so offensive.
Dioneo is like so offensive
Like I hate him so much
Like all their brains are like so dirty they need 100 maids to like
Clean it out, like fricking good maids.

LAURETTA
I'm still like so so upset, glad I had you guys there
for moral support.

EMILIA
Glad I got ma gurlsss

PAMPINEA
Ya we're your gurlsss :)

FILOMENA

Umm I'm feeling kinda dirty like from all those stories and
stuff,
Like I got rolled into
metaphorical mud
like maybe we should go cleanse ourselves?
Or something…

PAMPINEA

Ooo ya I love swimming.

(water appears and ladies are feelin itttt.)

LAURETTA

Ugh do you guys ever feel like so fat..like so fat
You're gunna float away like a hot air balloon,
Like so pretty and yellow and kid friendly?
Cause sometimes I get so scared.

PAMPINELLA

Omg you are not fatttt!

EMILIA

Ya you are so not fat stop being such a dumb betchhhh

FILOMENA

Ya shut up Lauretta…I'm the fat one…
Ugh this is like embarrassing but sometimes
When I'm sewing bunny ears for my 12 baby cousins
I can like actually…feel my thighs touching!
Like what kind of a failure of womankind am I?
Like no wonder I'm still unmarried…
Panfilo probably knows I feel that..
That's why he doesn't wanna commit.

LAURETTA

You lookin sooo good Filomena,
Sure that's not the reason why.

FILOMENA

Ya, then what is it??

LAURETTA

I don't know…maybe um your sewing isn't good enough
The key to a man's heart is through sewing.

EMILIA

Sooo deeep, deep like this water

PAMPINEA

You're deep Emilia,
Your water metaphors are to be envied.

EMILIA

I envy yo face… ;)

FILOMENA

Can you guys just shut up?
Also Emilia and Pampinea…you two are being so weirddd.
We're supposed to be cleansing OK!
Cleansing everything away till we're just pure,
Till we're one with the water.
Like you talking is just like ruining it.

LAURETTA

The water kinda feels like cinnamon buns

EMILIA

To me if feels like a water themed hug

FILOMENA

Shut the FUCK UP!

OTHER LADIES

....

(shift later in the day.)

FILOMENA

That was an
Interestinggggg
Story… Some Pg-13 moments
Def…
(I feel like I should have gotten my mom's permission.)

FILOSTRATO

I think you're old
Enough to not neeeed it ;)

FILOMENA

How are you finding your time in the fields?
Do you find it pleasing?

FILOSTRATO

Totes.
I did an oil painting of the sun setting yesterday-
And like it was so attractive I couldn't even
Look at it too long, I think I find a new calling-
I could show it to you if you want

FILOMENA

Ehhhh I good.
Oil paintings bore meeeee.
I prefer to listen to music.
I loveeeee music :)

FILOSTRATO

Oh so interesting, um give me a sec, BRB

(FILOSTRATO comes back with LAURETTA, he whispers something to her and sits down next to FILOMENA.)

LAURETTA (singing)
Love is like a meadow,
That won't shut up, it goes on and on and on and on
And that is how I feel about you
Like my love is so eco-friendly
Like it's like the ground, like no need to recycle,
It's just of the earth
My love is vegan, my love is puuuure
My love is eco-friendly,
I lovvvve you oh I love you so much I can't even
Filostratoooo you're so hottttt,
Let's makeoutt, makeout with me, not herrr,
Your hair is so perff

FILOSTRATO
Kk cool, that's um good for now. Byeeeee

(FILOSTRATO shoos LAURETTA off the stage. One of them throws a one-dollar bill at her, it was pretty good though right, she deserves dat??)

FILOSTRATO
I love music also,
Just makes a normal day like
So much better than that, like that
Normal day can suck it.

FILOMENA

Yes, that was very nice.
Thank you for that.
Was very pleasing to the ear,
Maybe the end was a bit odd though…

FILOSTRATO

Ya, musicians are hard to understand sometimes, weird,
How's um stuff with Panfilo? I saw him
Stare
At this butterfly for like 20 mins yesterday,
Was so weird.

FILOMENA

Not that weird,
He just appreciates nature and shit.
Ya we're good,
last night
We had a candlelit dinner outside
While he serenaded me
And all these frogs like legit danced for our love,
Was preti cuteeeee.

FILOSTRATO

I feel things so much you know, like sometimes
I think about my exxxes and they make me so upset
Cause they're all bitches and all cheated on me
And just sucked at existing and
Like they didn't appreciate LOVE
As a concept
And
And
I just don't think he's right for you

FILOMENA

Why not??

FILOSTRATO

I dunno like
I burn for you,
like at night.
I can't even feel ma limbs, they feel like
Trader Joes ghost pepper salsa,
Like so organic and trendy yet on fire
And he's just so content and shit
like staring at butterflies
and smoking pot and stuff.
Likeeee does HE EVEN HAVE ANY GOALS?
Cause I have about 13 and a half sooo

FILOMENA

He has plenty of goals and shitt,
Like um that's part of living
like having goals
And shit,
Also like we really shouldn't be talking for so long
Alone,
Like I'm a dignified and attractive young lady.

FILOSTRATO

But like…
Who cares though?
Like everyone's dead and dying
And stolen away by rabid guineas like everything's coming
apart
And isn't that kinda sexy sometimes?
Like if you don't think about it that hard,
Like nothinggg matters,
Like no one gives a fuck what you do,
Like if I touched you would anyone notice?

FILOMENA

Like I think my BF would care but…
God you feel a lot-of things,
I find that erotic.
It is rare to find a gentleman of such passions,
Who just feels things
And doesn't numb his emotions.

FILOSTRATO

Thanksssss

FILOMENA

I wanted to get married so bad
Ya know?
Like I had this idea of my wedding and how
There would be all these goats in like
Dresses like running around in feminine goat glee
And I wanted the whole church to be filled with purple roses
That sprouted
Glitter and Hershey kisses and stuff and
And I wanted to have a dress that made other chicks
Commit suicide
Cause it made them feel fat
Like I looked so hot I changed the weather like I
Changed what time of DAY it wassss!
And Panfilo would just look at me and see me
And just know I was the only thing that ever mattered,
And we were perfect together like Mary Kate and Ashley
Olsen
Or a cow and choco milk.
But I just,
I'm starting to think,
I don't know if it's going to happen….
(he doesn't seem like he wants to.)

FILOSTRATO

What do you think would happen if we touched?
You didn't answer before.

FILOMENA

Ug I feel like I shouldn't,
But like we're all probs gunna die anyway
And I find you veri attractive right now um
Maybe my body would turn into flowers?
Maybe the world would open up?
Ugh I dunno, ugh this is bad,
I am the most refined out of my female friends!
I have to set an example…

FILOSTRATO

If we touched I think life as we know it
Would end,
I think goats would stomp all the day long,
Way more than for you and Panfilo
They'd stomp so hard.

*(FILOSTRATO kisses FILOMENA. Maybe
peppermint sticks rain down from the ceiling or
cartoon hearts, something very V-day 4th grade
throwback kinda vibe. PANFILO walks in and
sees them, he walks out again.)*

FILOMENA

Wow

FILOSTRATO

That wasn't so bad, now was it…

FILOMENA

I don't know what I'm doing

FILOSTRATO

That's ok
No one does
All the priests are prob dead anyway so confession isn't even
A thing anymore.

(They makeout more.)

Day 7- Too Hot to handle

(Everyone is gathered together.)

PANFILO (pissed but pretending to be fine)
Good morning friends,
I had such a great sleep last night,
Slept like a legit log, like so well rested
And excited to tell you all a story,
So this story is about a couple,
A couple so happy they usually are
The envy
Of all around them!
So happy reality TV producers wanted to film them
To see if they ever fight,
But they always said no
Cause they didn't care about money
They cared about love!
I shall act
and my dear lady, Filomena, will you act as well?

FILOMENA

Ya..uh sure.

(PANFILO gives Filomena a script.)

FILOMENA (as WOMAN)
We are in love, that is a positive thing in my life.

PANFILO (as MAN)

I feel the same.

FILOMENA (as WOMAN)

I love being in love, what a feeling!
I'm on fire with it, like it sometimes
Hurts my body,
Like a fat mosquito like ow
Is that too deep and poetic for you to handle,
That image?

PANFILO (as MAN)

No. I feeleth the same.

PANFILO

And the couple would feed each other root beer flavored pop
tarts
And at night they would give each other love hugs,
I mean that in a literal sense, a hug infused wit love,
So calm it down Dioneo!
And they were just so happy and found everything
They needed in their whole life,
They didn't need marriage or children or more goats,
Just pure pure pure love,
But then one day the woman got run over by a bus...the end.

DIONEO

What is a bus??

PANFILO

Like a moving vehicle or whatevs.

LAURETTA

That story was weird, like there was no causality
Or whatever, it just ended.

PANFILO

Your mom has no causality!
I KNOW WHAT YOU DID FILOMENA!
I Know what you did and ya DUMPED!

FILOMENA

No, no, alack alack!
I love you, Filostrato sucks!

(PANFILO starts leaving.)

Panfilo don't go.
If we were home, it would be all different.
I never would have done such a thing,
At home I suck on lollypops slowly
And hug babies and I'm like so perfect and shit
And I don't know why I did this,
Fricking meadow,
Fricking stories with erotic subtextttt,
OH ALACKKK!!
Without you I can't feel my body,
Like you're just the best thing that ever
Happened to me
And if you never ever want to get married
I will just live in sin forever
Just waiting for you,
Juat embroidering your face
Hoping you'll pick me,
Hoping you'll notice me
And forget about boring things
Such as finances and how we shall live.
And Oh Alackkk!
Filostrato means nothing to me,
I am but a poor defenseless thing
And he seduced me with his big words
And I didn't even know what happened,
Like it was like a bad porno I was watching

FILOMENA (cont)
And I wasn't even apart of it.
I don't even want to live anymore without you,
I want to like throw my body
In like fire,
Like a mud bath but more suicidal and less girly,
And I'd give up everything for you,
My maids, my makeup, my BlueApron subscription
If you would take me back
Ohhhhhhh I just can't bear itttt,
The idea of you leaving makes me whole body
Burn and itch and shutdown, like
It cannot work-like you broke me.
I am nothing without you,
Nothinggg nothing at allll

(PANFILO leaves.)

EMILIA
woahhhh

PAMPINEA
It's ok Filomena!
Don't you frettt
Let's do like a gurls night!
Like some pedis and drunk sewing and
Like butterfly catching!!

EMILIA
Into itttt

LAURETTA
Yassss

(GIRLS start doing each other's nails. Guys start drinking beer.)

PAMPINEA

So like watt happened wit Panfilo?
Like will you guys be ok??

FILOMENA

I dunno, like I made out with Filostrato
But it was like no bigs.

FILOSTRATO

It was a yes bigs though!
Cause like I love you Filomena,
Like I just want us to run away and start a new life
And I wanna watch you knit for hours
Cause your hands are cute.

PAMPINEA

Awwww cuteee.

EMILIA

You're cute.

PAMPINEA

(Ugh why did you just say that??? Eep)

EVERYONE

....

LAURETTA

What is happening now,
I do not knowwwww,
But let's all sing and make it lesss weirddd
Filostrato you're hotttt

PAMPINEA

Ugh nothing is turning out like I thought it wouldddd

EMILIA

It neva doesss.
Just kiss me ok.
Nothing matters anymore anyway.

(PAMPINEA and EMILIA start making out.)

FILOMENA

What are you two doing???

EMILIA

I dunno like being together,
Like in a sexy way.
Don't think about it that hard ok.

LAURETTA

But two women cannot be together in such a manner!
It's unheard of.

FILOMENA

Whatevs, I'm over it.
Back to meeeee.
I can't believe Panfilo dumped me,
But he comes from such a good family
And like we were gunna have a goat wedding.

FILOSTRATO

Shhh it's ok.
We can have goats at our wedding.

LAURETTA

What about our wedding Filostrato!
OUR WEDDINGOUR WEDDINGGGG!

(PANFILO walks back eating a tub of Ben and Jerry's.)

LAURETTA

Oh look what's happening,
It's your boyfriends mouth in my mouth!

*(LAURETTA and PANFILO start making out.
FILOMENA is freaked.)*

PAMPINEA

Wait um, somethings happening to my hands,
Like I think they're bleeding or something,
Like I can't do your nails anymore
Filomena, like something's wrong.

LAURETTA

Wait mine are too!

DIONEO

I feel really itchy all over.

PANFILO

I think I see a rainbow,
Also I think I'm paralyzed.

LAURETTA

My body feels like half-off chocolate pudding.

EMILIA

Shhh ma little popsicle just lie down.

DIONEO

Oh no Alack! What is happening!
We are so rich and shit,
Like this countryside area is so sterile.

PAMPINEA

Well I might have um found a guinea
In the forest and been cuddling with it,
Like its mouth was foaming a little
But it was so heartwarming!

FILOMENA

OMG Your love of animals
Has inflicted us all! Ug the fricking plague!

PANFILO

I've had an itch for a few days now
And my left leg
Has become green,
So please don't blame it all on sweet Pampinea.

EMILIA

Why didn't you say something?

PANFILO

I thought that would be like a TMI situation,
Like are we close enough to discuss
That kinda stuff?

FILOMENA

Ugh this is so lammmme!
Ughhh
We need helppp!
Ooo I forgot, we are all saved-
We have our patron saint Clarita,
Let's call her down!

FILOSTRATO

Oh we are saveddd!

(Suddenly CLARITA comes down from the sky.)

CLARITA

Good day, fair ladies and gents,
Did I hear you needed help??

FILOMENA

Oh yes, Clarita!
We are dying from the plague,
Please save us!

EMILIA

Yess please Clarita!

CLARITA

Well my fair ladies,
If you want to be saved from the boils and
Angst of the plague,
Just sew two hundred blankets
Of ma face within ten minutes
And that will shift the world's balance.

PAMPINEA

But I cannot feel my body, how can I sew-eth?

CLARITA

Or um… smile very hard and
The symptoms should go away
Quickly.

(The LADIES smile and nothing happens.)

FILOMENA

Ugh none of this is helping!
Oh please Clarita,
We have pledged our lives to your care,
Please save us!

CLARITA

I'm sorry sweet ladies,
That's all the advice I have!
Clarita out!

> *(Suddenly the whole stage bursts on fire, then it becomes filled with pink glitter, then tubs of ice cream appear and the actors all eat it.)*

PAMPINEA

How long do we have??

EMILIA

Not long I don't think…

DIONEO

I'm gunna miss you guysss

ALL

Samee.

> *(All characters die. Maybe a live guinea pig runs around the stage for a bit then exits)*

THE END!

www.ingramcontent.com/pod-product-compliance
Lightning Source LLC
Chambersburg PA
CBHW031218120626
46545CB00003B/899